"This boo[illegible] tips on v[illegible] stones unturned so you will walk away with the answers to questions you did not even know you needed to ask. You will keep, refer to and lend this book as an excellent reference."

Janis Dietz, Ph.D.

"Writing your first book is challenge enough without worrying about technical stuff, such as 'When does a pamphlet become a book? How do you best use Amazon to promote and sell your book? How do you get ISBN numbers?

"Nancy Jones smartly capitalizes on her experiences from writing her first book to produce a tightly-written guidebook for busy professionals who 'know' they have a book inside them just waiting to get into print. Having overcome numerous obstacles to produce my first book *Saving Mom & Dad…and You*, I compliment Nancy on producing this needed publication – and appreciate how her directions will help me produce my next book."

Robert J Cullen, CFP®, AEP

"Nancy presents a power-packed collection of practical wisdom that anyone thinking of writing a book will find valuable."

Richard S. Kahler, CFP®

"*So You Want to Publish Your Book* is an absolute must-read for new authors embarking on the joyous insanity of writing a book! It's also required reading for published authors like me who want to re-launch their book and/or embark on their next writing project with greater organization, forethought, and rationality. Nancy has created a one-stop guide, tutor, and FAQ list for people who yearn to get their voice into the reading marketplace. She could well have sub-titled it Everything You Always Wanted to Know About Book Writing and Publishing but Didn't Know the Questions to Ask. Read this book, keep it by your word processor, writing desk, or vintage Selectric, and consult it often."

Edward Jacobson, Ph.D

So You Want to

Publish Your Book

So You Want to

Publish Your Book

Your Guide to Self-Publishing Nonfiction

Nancy Langdon Jones, CFP®

AdvisorPress
Sunnyvale, California

So You Want to Publish Your Book:
Your Guide to Self-Publishing Nonfiction

Nancy Langdon Jones, CFP®
http://www.nancysbooks.com
nancy@nancysbooks.com

AdvisorPress
http://www.advisorpress.com
1153 Bordeaux Drive, Suite 109
Sunnyvale, CA 94089
info@advisorpress.com
(408)400-0400

ISBN: 978-1-60353-017-0

$14.95

Printed in the United States of America

This book is dedicated to all you aspiring authors out there. May you publish and flourish!

Contents

Acknowledgments

There is no way this book could have been written without the help of an incredible number of generous, supportive individuals. There is likewise no way I could possibly thank all those involved! There are some, however, without whose affectionate nit-picking and nagging I could never have succeeded.

Thomas B. Hubbard, Dan Yoshimoto and **Debbie Galllant**, for their eagle eyes, relentless proofreading and scrupulous editing.

My many **friends** and **colleagues**, who selflessly shared their stories and experiences.

Peter W. Johnson, Jr. and **Mattias Bergman**, co-publishers.

And **Claude**, my wonderful husband, who gave me the time and space I needed and was always there with an encouraging word.

Preface

Writing a book was never on my bucket list…let alone publishing one. But after writing and co-publishing my first book in 2001, I was surprised by the number of would-be authors who approached me to ask how I'd done it.

Well, it wasn't easy back then. What a difference a few years has made! With the tools available today I honestly believe anyone who writes a book and doesn't at least consider self-publishing is missing out.

I'm hoping this book will help you realize your potential as publisher of your own work. I've tried to take you through the simple steps, one by one, so that you can easily get your book to market.

Last year I persuaded my husband to finish a work he'd had in progress for decades by promising to publish his book, *'Specially Not No Chocolate*. He called my bluff. It took less than a month, after he finished writing, to get the book proofed, printed, published and up on Amazon.

Publishing is easy. Marketing is hard!

Chapter One

Why?

Your response to this question is invaluable. Once you've seriously pondered this complex query you'll know not only why you're reading this book, but also why you're writing a book and for whom you're writing. Without this knowledge, why bother?

Perhaps you've discovered a brand-new concept and it's screaming to be revealed to the world. Do you want your words of wisdom to be available under your moniker to clients and prospects? Maybe you simply want your name on the cover of a book to impress family and friends. Whatever your personal reasons, it's important that you understand your motivations and take a realistic look at just why it is that you feel compelled to put pencil to paper…or type up a storm on your PC.

I certainly never set out to write a book[1] nor had any idea a book was in me. But now that it's a done deal I realize it's among the half dozen things in my life that I'm most proud to have accomplished.

For me it started on a Sunday afternoon.

The answers were already there. All they had to do was scroll down. But no, newbies to the website would just ask the same questions over and over.

I was moderating the 'Getting Started' discussion boards on *financial-planning.com* and decided to take an hour or two and write up a FAQ sheet to post on the site. It would have answers to the most-asked questions on how to become a financial planner. The hours turned into days as I realized it would take more than a couple of pages to answer the important questions fully. Perhaps a pamphlet? It took weeks of struggling to come up with concise answers to a myriad of issues before I became conscious of the fact that I needed to write an entire book.

And so began a yearlong chapter in my life that resulted in my first book, <u>So You Want to Be a Financial Planner: Your Guide to a New Career</u>.

---

[1] <u>So You Want to Be a Financial Planner: Your Guide to a New Career</u> was first published in September 2001 and is now in its fifth edition.

A couple of my clients were already published authors. Watching their faces light up as they talked about their work had always seemed pretty cool to me. But the idea of actually writing a book myself never occurred to me until I was in the middle of it.

It's a life-changing experience!

Since it was a niche, I knew who my readers would be prior to writing: students and career changers considering vocations as financial planners. A little research on Amazon at the time (circa 2000) told me there had been very little published on the topic.

Once I had my subject and knew for whom I was writing, I began to look for some help on how and where to start. I found an out-of-print book on Amazon that explained the steps to writing a nonfiction book and getting a publisher. The book urged me to write a proposal prior to doing anything else. Today you can just Google "How to Write a Book Proposal", and you'll have a selection of proposal formats at your disposal.

I was eager to get started writing, so that bit of advice was tough to follow, but I credit it with keeping me on track for the entire year of writing. Your proposal should include the following:

Overview

What your book is about and who you expect will buy it.

About the Author

Detailed information about you and why you are qualified to write your book. Make yourself look really good and credible.

The Market

To whom you plan to market and how you will reach your market.

The Competition

What other books are written on your topic and what makes yours better.

Annotated Table of Contents

Chapter titles with a paragraph describing what each chapter will contain.[2]

Sample Material

A page or chapter from your book to show your writing style.

Your proposal can be a dozen pages or a hundred pages, but more is not better. If you're looking for a publisher, they want the facts and won't have time to bother with a tome that's longer than your book will be. Just be certain to include the key elements

---

[2] This was the single most valuable part of the proposal for me. Keeping the chapters separate and knowing what I planned to include in each chapter made it much easier once I began writing. The entire Annotated Table of Contents from my proposal serves at the Table of Contents for my book, So You Want to Be a Financial Planner.

noted above, and concentrate on the sample material.

If you want more than free Internet suggestions for a proposal (probably a good idea if you've never written a proposal before), I recommend Stephen Blake Mettee's The Fast Track Course on How to Write a Nonfiction Book Proposal[3]. This 100-page quick read talks about much more than just the proposal.

Putting the proposal together will not only give you a jump-start on understanding your purpose and motivation for writing your book; it will give you a taste of what's in store for you during the writing process. Both take a tremendous amount of discipline. Think back to your college days and try to remember what it was like writing those wretched term papers due weeks or months from the assignment date. There was always tomorrow to start the research and so much other stuff to do today.

Get out your annotated Table of Contents and your calendar. Pencil in work for each chapter and reasonable dates for completion. Carve out uninterrupted times that you will work on your book. Try to allow blocks of several hours or even entire days so you can

---

[3] Stephen Blake Mettee's The Fast Track Course on How to Write a Nonfiction Book Proposal, Quill Driver Books, April 2008.

concentrate on nothing but research or writing during those times.

If you've already written your book, congratulations! I still recommend writing the proposal. You'll need it if you're sending your manuscript off to a publisher. It will also help you with the most difficult challenge you have ahead: Marketing.

Chapter Two

Marketing

The first thing you need to know about marketing your book is that your publisher isn't going to. Your publisher's job is to get the books to market. The rest is up to you.

For whom are you writing this book? Think long and hard on this question, even before you begin. Do you just want the personal pleasure and satisfaction of writing a book, or do you have information to disseminate that will change the world as we know it?

Might as well face the fact that unless you're John Grisham, or his ilk, your book, no matter how good it is, will NOT be for everyone.

Knowing who will be reading your book will help you write it from the first word. Picture your audience as you write and by the time you finish you'll have a pretty good idea how to reach your market. Find your niche and go for it.

In today's publishing world, your mailing list and Amazon are the two must-haves to market your book.

Mailing List

Get out your client list, your colleague list, your vendor list, your Christmas card list, your alumni list, your Facebook contacts, your list of family and friends, and your list of anyone and everyone you ever met at a party or professional gathering. The reason that you need these lists is because the more people who know about your book, the more potential you have for selling it!

Make up fliers and mail or email information about your book and where it can be purchased to absolutely everyone you can think of, even if they were just a passing acquaintance. You never know. Maybe they know someone for whom your book was written. You may want to design different fliers for different groups: something more professional for clients and business contacts and more personal for friends and family. But get *something* out to as many people as you can muster.

Also, within these lists will be people to whom you'll want to send review copies. Compose a nice letter to send out with the book, telling them how much you appreciate their taking the time to read the book. Ask these people, if they like your book, to post a positive review for you on Amazon, Barnes & Noble, and anywhere else they can manage. They do not have to purchase your book on these venues in order to post a review, but they do need to have made *some* purchase from the site. It's simple! In your letter you might even explain how easy it is to write a review in Microsoft Word, then cut and paste it into the appropriate place. Send your reviewers the link to your book site on Amazon and anywhere else you want reviews to appear.

While you're preparing lists, be sure to create one that includes libraries, newspaper contacts and any other media, particularly in your area. I would have suggested putting Oprah on the list, but unsolicited books are no longer accepted, according to her website.

Amazon.com

The behemoth. You *must* be on Amazon if you expect to sell your book. Most self-publishing houses will set you up with Ingram, the largest book wholesaler in the United States, who will see that your book is available print-on-demand to Amazon and other booksellers. But just because your book shows up there doesn't mean you're marketing it. Working with Amazon is practically a business in itself!

Volumes have been written about how to work with Amazon, so I won't go into too much detail here. Still, you must understand that your book page on Amazon is a quarry waiting to be mined.

One of my favorite books regarding working with Amazon is Brent Sampson's Sell Your Book on Amazon.[4] In a well organized 160 or so pages, Sampson takes the reader through the confusing world of Amazon, explaining the new language involved with navigating the site and getting exposure for your book. He suggests publishing through a well-researched POD (print-on-demand) service as the easiest way to get listed on Amazon. Look for a POD service that uses EDI (electronic data interchange) distribution, and preferably has a relationship with Ingram.

Once your book is listed there are numerous things you can do to promote it on the Amazon website, or at least make it more visible to potential buyers. Sampson starts with helping you complete your Author Profile

---

[4] Brent Sampson's Sell Your Book on Amazon, Outskirts Press, March 2007.

Page and build your Book Detail Page. For instance, letting visitors to your page 'Search Inside' can give them more information to help them decide to make a purchase. Another great tip that Sampson recommends is utilizing the 'Tell a Friend' feature to send the link to your Book Detail Page to anyone on any of your lists. The more the merrier!

Another interesting book, one that should probably be read even before writing your book, is Aiming at Amazon by Aaron Shepard.[5] Subtitled "The NEW Business of Self Publishing or How to Publish Books for Less, Sell Without Hassle, and Double Your Profit (or More) With Print on Demand and Book Marketing on Amazon.com", Aiming at Amazon delivers on its title. I advise reading this book before writing because of all the great information Shepard has about actually writing the book in the proper format and including a PDF version. In a chapter entitled 'Building Your Book' he takes you step by step through doing just that.

Steve Weber's Plug Your Book: Online Book Marketing for Authors[6] is filled with valuable information on how to use Amazon's website to your advantage, including

---

[5] Aaron Shepard's Aiming at Amazon, Shepard Publications, January 2007.

[6] Steve Weber's Plug Your Book! Online Book Marketing for Authors, Book Publicity through Social Networking, Weber Books, February 2007.

detailed instructions on how to encourage Amazon's top reviewers to review your book. It's incredibly easy! Just go to www.amazon.com/gp/customer-reviews/top-reviewers.html and find reviewers who are willing to post their email addresses and who like to review books similar to the one you have written. Some of them are very specific in their tastes, so don't waste their time and your rejection. Be as personable and complimentary as you can be in the letter you send to the reviewers you select. A tip is to start at the low end where reviewers may be eager to get more books under their top reviewer belt. Read the profile and send your request to as many reviewers as possible. Some will respond.

Weber goes way beyond Amazon and includes specific advice on how to build your own website and ventures into blogging and social networking as a means to sell your book.

Media Kit

You'll need one. A media kit can be your foot in the door for media reviews, speaking engagements, radio and TV interviews and other things that will help sell your book.

You wrote it! You're the expert! Take advantage of the fact and spell it out in your media kit, which should contain your credentials, photos, book cover, reviews, availability, awards, interviews, other publications and everything wonderful about you.

In The Frugal Book Promoter: How to Do What Your Publisher Won't[7], Carolyn Howard-Johnson takes you through the process of developing and enhancing your media kit. This is an ongoing endeavor that will improve, once you have new and better publicity (clippings, recent interviews, book signings, etc.) to include.

Your media kit is an entry to speaking engagements, and speaking engagements are great ways to promote your book.

Most of this is self-evident, but if you want in-depth advice and instructions on putting your media kit together, Howard-Johnson goes so far as recommending font size, and includes sample media release and query pages. Furthermore, she helps you develop a contact list where you can send your media kit (librarians, bookstores, newspapers, TV and radio stations, etc.) and suggests venues for speaking engagements (professional or charitable organizations, libraries, corporations, etc.) Consider speaking to college classes, if your book contains information pertinent to the curriculum.

---

[7] Carolyn Howard-Johnson's The Frugal Book Promoter: How to Do What Your Publisher Won't Star Publish, July 2004.

Other parts of her book deal with writers' conferences, designing your website, publisher's contracts, cover design and so much more!

While Howard-Johnson merely touches on Amazon, her book is a good anthology of stuff you could/should do to promote your book, and as the title promises, it's mostly free or low cost.

Chapter Three

Print on Demand

Bingo! ePublishing for Dummies®[8]. The familiar black and yellow paperback called out to me from the rack at Border's. Suddenly I knew my book had to be in electronic format so it could be read on a computer and the links could be followed. I could publish and print it myself as I received orders from anyone wanting the print version.

It was spring of 2001 and POD (print-on-demand) for books was still in its infancy. I'd never even heard of it. My book dealt with a rapidly growing industry, where changes were occurring every day. How great it would be to revise content one day

[8] Victoria Rosenborg's ePublishing for Dummies®, IDG Books Worldwide, Inc., 2001.

and send the very next book out with the new material.

I'd sent my manuscript to half a dozen publishers. Despite letters of introduction from respected industry professionals and repeated phone calls and emails, I hadn't heard a peep from any of them. Now I knew why: I was meant to learn about ePublishing and print-on-demand.

Digital vs. Offset

Traditionally, books were published using offset printing, where an inked image is transferred (offset) from a plate to a rubber blanket, then to the printing surface[9]. Today there is a choice between offset and digital printing, the reproduction of digital images on a physical surface. Making that choice most often boils down to money. Set up costs for offset printing can be $1000 or more. The same book can be digitally ready to print for under $50. However, the unit cost for the offset print book is considerably less than the unit cost of a digitally print book. If you feel your book will sell 1000 or fewer copies, then digital is the way to go. More than 1000 copies, you should consider offset printing. At 2000 copies the cost of offset printing goes down dramatically.

---

[9] Wikipedia

Around 650 copies is probably a break-even rule of thumb.

In making your decision, consider whether you expect to have frequent changes or new editions to your nonfiction book which may make digital printing more attractive from a cost perspective.[10]

ePublishing

ePublishing is simply having your book in an eBook format, such as a PDF[11] file, that can be transmitted electronically. Once you have a PDF file of your book, it can be sent out to view on a computer or other media, or you can send the file to a printer to have print copies made. One feature of the eBook is that Internet links within the book can be made live. The reader on a computer can click on the link and go directly to a website. My book, So You Want to Be a Financial Planner, contains over 200 links to websites. I offer purchasers a free download of the PDF file to make it easier for them to go directly to the sites.

Once the printer has a PDF file of the book, it can be printed in hardbound or soft cover,

[10] I chose digital printing for my book because changes in my industry are frequent and I wanted to be able to update quickly.

[11] Portable Document Format

a single copy or thousands; whatever is ordered. Thus you have "print-on-demand".

Print-On-Demand

Print-on-demand means no inventory, no storage facility, no up-front big-bucks investment, no distribution problems and no staff to package orders. Your POD company theoretically takes care of all that for you. Per book printing costs may be a little higher than bulk printing, but believe me, unless you're pretty sure you can sell thousands of books you'll be much happier having them printed to order. With a POD company you can order one book or hundreds at a time, depending on your need.

POD Publishers vs. POD Printers

POD publishers offer a package of services, which generally includes up-front costs for layout, choice of cover design and minimal marketing and distribution. As with any legal arrangement, check your agreement or contract thoroughly. Know who owns the copyright and the cover art and what you can take with you if you decide later on to use a different publishing company or to self-publish.

A POD printing company takes your completed manuscript in an acceptable form to fit into their template and prints it. You are the publisher and retain all the rights.

The POD printing company I use is Lightning Source, Inc[12]. Their procedure was easy and painless and went exactly as explained on their website. My experience publishing my husband's book, 'Specially Not No Chocolate! went like this:

1. He wrote the book and a friend designed the cover for us.
2. We opened an account with Lightning Source, Inc at no cost and submitted a PDF file of the book. There was a small set-up fee.
3. We hired a graphic artist to fit the cover into the Lightning Source template.[13]
4. Lightning Source sent us a proof copy for $30. We received the proof just a couple days after ordering it. We made some changes, resubmitted the edited copy and purchased a second proof.
5. We accepted the second proof and Lightning Source made the title available to book buyers including

[12] www.lightningsource.com

[13] I think with a little more courage and experimentation we could have eventually figured this out for ourselves and saved the expense.

Internet retailers such as Amazon.com[14].

6. We ordered 100 copies at a discount to sell from our website and distribute to friends, family and contributors.

7. We set the book up on our website for sale and notified those to whom we'd been marketing that it was finally available.

The entire process took only a couple of weeks (once the book was written and ready to submit to Lightning Source) and cost less than $1000[15], including the graphic artist, who accounted for more than half the cost.

Now that the print book is accessible through Lightning Source, we can order copies whenever we want and send revisions or updates to the original copy at any time for a small set-up fee.

Next we went to Amazon.com and downloaded the digital version into Kindle. We also offer a PDF file from our website to buyers who just want to download the book to their computers. Of course they don't get

---

[14] Lightning Source, Inc is a subsidiary of Ingram Industries, Inc. Ingram Book Group is the world's largest wholesale distributor of book product.

[15] Graphic artist was $600. The "under $1000" costs included the graphic artist, ISBN, set up fees, two proof copies, etc., and the initial order of 100 books.

an autographed copy the way buyers of the print version do when they purchase from our website!

Chapter Four

Putting Your Book Together

Once you have your proposal finished it's time to get serious about writing. With today's word processing programs (primarily Microsoft Word) you can turn out a perfectly respectable script that can translate into a PDF file accepted by almost any publisher.

Word Processor or Publishing Software?

Bottom line, you want your finished product to look professional. Should you put out $700 or more for proper desktop publishing software, such as Adobe's InDesign, or will your word processor do the trick? The main difference is page layout. Publishing software considers one page at a time and how it looks, whereas word processors look at the entire document without regard for appropriate page breaks and typography. Your budget and learning curve should be taken into account when you make this decision. Word will certainly get you by, but is it suitable for your market? Probably.

In his wonderfully comprehensive work, Book Design and Production: A Guide for Authors and Publishers[16], Pete Masterson spends an entire chapter explaining how to change the default settings in Word to make the layout as professional as possible, even though he strongly urges authors to use publishing software instead of word processing.

Preparing and Designing the Manuscript

Per the Library of Congress, your book will need at least 49 pages to be considered a book. Otherwise, you've written a brochure or a pamphlet. Next to decide is trim size. Your book can be anything from a large coffee table size to a small pocketbook. Unless you need the space for graphs and charts or specialized artwork, sticking to standard sizes will save you time and money. For instance, digest size (5 3/8 x 8 3/8 or 5 ½ x 8

---

[16] Pete Masterson's Book Design and Production: A Guide for authors and Publishers, Aeonix Publishing Group, December 2007. There is also a wealth of information on the Aeonix Publishing Group home page at www.aeonix.com.

½ inches) will allow you to print 2 pages on a standard 8 ½ x 11 paper. This is good for both checking your work to see how it will look on the page printed from your printer and keeping costs down with your printing company.

You'll have other decisions to make as well, such as whether to justify margins or leave the right margin "ragged". Will you indent paragraphs or use block style? Your selection of fonts is practically limitless. Do you plan on playing it safe, or will you strike out with an unusual font? Best to stick with a serif font that will be easier to read, and use san serif for headings. Still, the possibilities are vast!

Inside the Book

Most nonfiction books have three basic parts: the front matter, the main text and the reference material.

The front matter is often numbered with Roman numerals. Sometimes there will be a page or two of testimonials just inside the cover. Otherwise, the very first right hand page inside the cover is called the "half title page" and consists of *only* the title. No subtitle, no author name, no nothing except the title. The left side (back of the half title page) is left blank.

The next right hand page is the title page, which includes the full title and sub-title of the book and both the author's and publisher's names. On the back of the title page is the copyright page, where you can find the copyright information, printing dates, name and address of the publisher, ISBN[17] and other notes.

If you will have a dedication, preface and/or acknowledgments, which are optional, they follow the copyright page.

The table of contents comes next, followed by more optional pages, such as a foreword by someone other than the author, and/or introduction (notes) by the author. This completes the front matter and if you were using Roman numerals they would end here.

The main text generally begins on a right hand page and if you change your numbering system this would be Arabic numeral 1, though the number is often suppressed on the first page of chapter one.

The reference material contains the appendix and index, if either is to be present.

Cover

The cover is a whole other experience! Its importance cannot be emphasized enough!

---

[17] See Chapter 5.

The cover is the first thing a potential buyer sees and the sale can be made or lost right there. First impressions *do* matter! Picture your cover the size of a postage stamp on Amazon.com. Is it legible? Think of it on a bookstore shelf. Will it stand out? Your title should be big enough to be read even on that Amazon display. That's just for the front cover.

The spine carries the title (with the top of the letters near the front cover), your name (often just your last name) and the publisher's name or logo.

The back cover is vitally important as well, particularly if your book will be sold at conferences or in bookstores where potential buyers will pick it up and turn it over. Isn't that the first thing you do when you're looking for a new book? The back is filled with a wealth of information and it's the best place for you to make the sale. Tell your buyer why they need your book. Give them a list of benefits they can't refuse, along with two or three resounding endorsements or testimonials that will let your buyer know they can't go another minute without reading your book.

Other things that go on the back are the price of the book (another decision you'll have to wrestle with), the bar code[18] with your ISBN and maybe your picture.

If you have money to spend, this is the place to spend it – on the cover. Even if you don't plan to have artwork on your cover, a good graphic artist can place the title and other information in a professional manner and fit it into your printer's template.

Editing

I cannot say enough about having good editors and/or proofreaders. It shouldn't just be you! Your editors should be with you every step of the way going over every word and idea. Sloppy grammar, misspelled words and sentences that make no sense will destroy your readership faster than anything else. Even if you have vitally important information to impart, if your readers are distracted by careless content they will not buy your book nor appreciate the work you've done.

---

[18] See Chapter 5.

Chapter Five

The Dreaded Technical Stuff

If you don't have the expertise, don't worry! Help is available in the form of websites, students, neighbors and many others.

Editing

Warning: Don't do this alone! A good editor is crucial to your work. Judges say that defendants who choose to represent themselves have a fool for a client. Don't let that be said of you in reference to your writing. You're probably too close to your work to catch the many faux pas that are inherent in any rough manuscript. Of course, your writing should be in as great shape as possible before sending it off to an editor. Now is the time for all those great grammatical things we learned in English class to pop back into focus. Problem is, many of the rules have changed since most of us were in the sixth grade.

One thing (of many) I found that I was doing wrong, was hitting the space bar twice after each sentence, just as I was taught to do in typing class. Well, modern computers make that unnecessary. If you do it, you will mess up otherwise fine computer spacing and your manuscript won't look as nice. There's an easy fix with Word by using the "find function" in your "edit" drop-down menu. Hit the space bar twice. Find all the double spaces you've made and replace them with a single space. You can do your entire document by using "replace all".

If you want to learn a lot about editing and have fun learning, do yourself a favor and pick up a copy of Carolyn Howard-Johnson's delightful book, The Frugal Editor.[19] As the title suggests, it shouldn't cost you an arm and a leg to edit. Much, if not all of the work can be done yourself, if you're meticulous and pay attention to her myriad recommendations for preparing your book for publication.

After reading her book and making corrections, if you want an editor, she gives you

---

[19] Carolyn Howard-Johnson's The Frugal Editor: Put Your Best Book Forward to Avoid Humiliation and Ensure Success.

ideas on where to find one. If you're feeling thrifty, check the writing departments at local colleges and universities, or ask for help from literary friends. Be sure to recognize the people who help you on your acknowledgments page!

Ideally, your editor should be with you from the beginning, so they can understand your style and help you avoid future errors as you complete your work.

ISBN/Bar Code

The ISBN (International Standard Book Number) is a thirteen-digit identifier unique to every book. There used to be only ten digits in the ISBN but in 2007 they expanded to thirteen, by adding a "978" prefix. That is why you'll see two numbers on some books: ISBN-10 and ISBN-13.

The ISBN comes first because it is an integral part of the bar code. You can purchase a single ISBN from www.myidentifiers.com for $125. The bar code is $25 more. Go to www.isbn.org/standards/home/isbn/us/application.asp to purchase a block of ten numbers for $245 (plus $25 for each barcode). Each version of your book must have its own ISBN, so if you're planning to have an eBook (which doesn't need a bar code) or publish in audio format or expect a second edition, it would be wise to have the extra ISBNs on hand.

The ISBN and Bookland EAN bar code[20] need to be placed on the back cover of your book, so you'll need this information prior to your cover designer finishing the cover design. Some POD publishers offer to acquire the ISBN and bar code for you, or will take your ISBN and incorporate it into the bar code for an extra fee.

BISAC

This is the little reference code up in the left hand corner of the back of the book cover that lets librarians and bookstore clerks know where to display your book most appropriately. It's an acronym for Book Industry Systems Advisory Committee. Go to www.bisg.org/bisac/subjectcodes to find a list of codes.

Seller's Permit

Will you be selling books from your website or retail within your state? If so, and if your state charges sales tax, then you must collect sales tax for print copies of your book sold in your state. This seller's permit is actually

[20] The Bookland EAN is an international barcode used to identify books and other items. It includes the ISBN as well as the currency and price of the book.

a resale permit. You will be buying your book to resell to others. You don't have to pay sales tax on the books you purchase to resell. But you won't be able to purchase those books without paying sales tax, unless your seller's permit is on file with the company from which you're buying your book. Catch 22! Get the permit.

In most states that charge sales tax, you can register in one of three ways: in person at a field office of the taxing authority, by mail, or by downloading an application from the Internet and either taking it to a field office or returning it by mail. Once you have the permit, you will be required to send a copy of it to the company (printer or POD publisher) in order to purchase your books wholesale.

If you tell the taxing authority that you are just starting out and don't expect to sell many books in your state you may be able to avoid making a deposit and can file annually. Google "state sales tax" and the name of your state to learn how to get the permit in your state.

Business License

Depending upon where you live, you may be required to obtain a business license before actively engaging in the business of selling your book. I used to live in an unincorporated area of a large county and did not have a business license. When I moved to a small incorporated city, they notified me that I would need a license. They had shared information with the state taxing authority and knew I was paying sales tax, thus in business. It didn't matter that I have no retail traffic and sell my books 100% online. The fact that I was in business made it mandatory to register and increase the city coffers.

You may be required to obtain a DBA ("Doing Business As" fictitious business name), particularly if you are not using your own name as your business name. You will also need your DBA or the name of your business for your merchant account.

Merchant Account

If you will be selling books from your personal website or at workshops and conferences, you will need a merchant account to process orders paid with credit cards. Merchant accounts have become highly competitive in recent years so do some shopping around for good rates. Most merchant accounts include Visa and MasterCard, and make Discover and American Express available through special arrangements.

One place to begin looking for a merchant account might be the bank where you have your business checking account. Compare rates and convenience with online merchant accounts and those offered through discount membership warehouses such as Costco and Sam's Club. I have been pleased with my experience using Cardservice International and Authorize.net through Wells Fargo, but found the best rates with Elevon through Costco, so I recently made the change.

You will pay a fixed monthly fee for a shopping cart and processing fees (around $50-75), small per-transaction charges and a percentage of the sale to the respective card company. You will be notified via email each time a transaction occurs and the sale will be credited to your checking account.

Checking Account

Whether you receive royalties and/or direct payment through a merchant account or retail sales at conferences and workshops, you will need a separate bank account for your book earnings and expenses. Sales from your merchant account will go directly into your designated checking account and fees will be deducted.

Keeping this accounting separate from your personal banking, right from the start, will serve you well down the line. If you are a sole proprietor, acting under your own name or a DBA, you will file a Schedule C with your income tax return. Trust me, having this information in its own account will save you many headaches!

Copyright

Your book, technically, is copyrighted once it's been written. Be sure and put the information on your copyright page, using the symbol © or "copyright" and the date of publication. However, it costs only $35[21] and filling out a one-page form to copyright your work. It's worth it, just in case. If it's your work, you don't want someone else making claim to it.

Navigate to www.copyright.gov and read the instructions. You'll need to register to get a user ID and password, then fill out a brief form (Form TX) and send two copies of your book to the Library of Congress copyright office. I received my copyright registration in about three months, but a much longer wait time is not uncommon.

Index

If your book is nonfiction, it should have an index. There's a learning curve to create the index using Word, and it's time consuming, but your work will be taken much more se-

---

[21] As of this writing the cost of copyrighting a book was $35 online and $45 to print out the form and mail it in.

riously if it includes an index. Take the time to generate the index or hire someone to do it for you. You'll be glad you did!

Chapter Six

Authors Who Have Done It

And now some stories from people just like you who felt they had a book in them and finally took the bull by the horns and began writing.

Richard S. Kahler, CFP®, ChFC
Kahler Financial Group
Rapid City, SD

Tell us about your business.

I am a fee-only financial planner with a solo practice. My firm, Kahler Financial Group, serves seventy families and has a support staff of three. My average account as of 12/31/08 was $1.6 million. Our average client is a business owner, professional, or retiree. Over 40% of our clients live outside the state of South Dakota. In 2008 Wealth Manager named us the largest financial planning firm in our six state area.

In 1995 I became interested in the "emotional side" of money and joined the Nazrudin project, a leaderless think-tank of financial planners, coaches, and therapists. In 2000 I attended George Kinder's two-day workshop, the Seven Stages of Money Maturity. Shortly thereafter, I pioneered a financial therapy workshop with Dr. Ted Klontz at Onsite Workshops outside of Nashville, TN. Our program was featured in the Wall Street Journal

My books came out of this work and the prompting of reporters wondering, "Where is the book?"

Tell us about your book(s).

The Financial Wisdom of Ebenezer Scrooge: 5 Principles to Transform Your Relationship with Money

Ebenezer Scrooge would seem an unlikely source from which to glean financial wisdom. However, Dickens' classic tale of how Scrooge left behind his miserly ways and transformed into a joyful, compassionate and generous man is a powerful model for transforming our relationship with money that we all can benefit from today. Also now available in paperback! Published by HCI 2006/2008

Facilitating Financial Health: Tools for Financial Planners, Coaches, and Therapists

This book is an essential resource for financial professionals. It provides cutting-edge tools to help clients transform money from a major source of stress to a valued resource for building more satisfying lives. Published by NUCO 2008

Conscious Finance: Uncover Your Hidden Money Beliefs and Transform the Role of Money in Your Life

Although it includes essential information on investing, budgeting, estate planning, and asset protection, this book goes far beyond strategies for solving immediate money problems. Its goal is to help readers build a healthy relationship with money in which it is a trusted and valuable servant rather than their master or their enemy. Published by FoxCraft 2005/2007

Wired for Wealth: Change Your Money Mindset and Unleash Your Wealth Potential (Coming soon!)

Neuroscience and money are being bandied about from Wall Street to Main Street, with people realizing that what goes on in their brain directly impacts their bank account. As financial stress mounts and an economic crash looms, the Wired for Wealth authors show that the biggest threat to your financial health is not a recession, it's your mindset. Published by HCI 2009

Do you have a dedicated website for your book(s)? What's the address?

www.consciousfinance.com

www.financialwisdomofscrooge.com

www.facilitatingfinancialhealth.com

www.wiredforwealth.com

What percentage of time do you spend each month dealing with book business?

I spend very little time, maybe 1%.

Which came first, the book or the publisher?

Instances where the book came first: Conscious Finance, The Financial Wisdom of Ebenezer Scrooge, Facilitating Financial Health.

The publisher asked that we do a sequel to The Financial Wisdom of Ebenezer Scrooge, so that is what prompted Wired For Wealth and the second edition of The Financial Wisdom of Ebenezer Scrooge, which was printed with a new cover and in paperback.

How did you find a publisher?

For The Financial Wisdom of Ebenezer Scrooge, we used the publishing company owned by a friend of my co-author.

For Facilitating Financial Health we were introduced to the publisher by a fellow author. The publisher heard a presentation done by Dr. Ted Klontz and myself and signed us shortly thereafter.

What was the most valuable thing you learned in your research process?

I learned that it's hard to get a publisher interested if you've published fewer than three books. Also, I learned that you write because of passion for your subject, not for the money. In fact, it actually takes money to write a book. I've finally broken even on the books I've written!

What's it like dealing with your publisher?

In some cases, it's been very frustrating. One publisher left off the endorsements, misrepresented the copyright, and used incredibly inferior materials to print the first edition. While they eventually made things right, it was a very frustrating experience.

I've found all our publishers helpful in sending out promotional copies of our books to the media. However, I've also learned that one better not expect a publisher to do any marketing, they won't. If you don't have a game plan on how YOU are going to promote and market your book, it's not going to happen.

If you set up your own publishing company, please explain the steps you took. Would you do it again?

For Conscious Finance, Kathleen Fox and I researched printers and a graphic artist. Kathleen did all the typesetting. We make much more per book off of Conscious Finance than any of my published books. Indeed I would self-publish again.

Who did the technical stuff (copyright, ISBN, cover art, editing)?

My co-author did the editing and ISBN. We hired a graphic artist, and I did the copyright.

Do you have a merchant account? How does that work?

No.

Describe your market and how you reach them.

Our market is people interested in personal finance and self-help along with professionals (financial planners, therapists, and financial coaches). I promote my books through speaking engagements, websites, columns, my practice, and interviews.

As I've said before, do not lull yourself into thinking for one moment that a publisher is going to market the book. To that end, you are almost better publishing yourself.

What a publisher will do is give you a little push to their distributors and get you in a few bookstores you would have on your own. Being with a publisher makes it far easier for resellers and bookstores to carry your book, once they are interested in your book because of your efforts.

So, it's up to you.

If starting out now, what would you do differently?

I would not have followed Dan Poynter's[22] advice. It was worthless for us.

---

[22]Dan Poynter is the author of Dan Poynter's Self-Publishing Manual and many other books dealing with publishing.

What's the best advice you can give someone wanting to sell his or her first book?

Approach your mother, first. She will probably buy one!

You need to relentlessly push out emails to reporters, broadcasters, writers, etc. You need to give speeches, do seminars where you can have back of the room sales. If you have a day job, I would suggest hiring a PR person to keep you in front of the media. Work, Work, Work.

Here is the sad reality: 10% of the work in writing a book is in writing it, 90% of the work is in marketing it.

Robert J. Cullen, CFP®
Retirement Planning and Management Group
Upland, CA

Tell us about your business.

I provide specialized financial planning services for elderly individuals in declining health. Myths and half-truths abound in this arena. I chose to write a book to dispel these myths and promote my business.

Tell us about your book(s).

Saving Mom & Dad…And You is written for consumers and professionals not familiar with long-term care issues. The heart of the book is a proprietary system for grouping assets and income that simplifies understanding of the eligibility rules for Medi-Cal (Medicaid).

Do you have a dedicated website for your book(s)? What's the address?

http://www.savingmomanddad.com/

What percentage of time do you spend each month dealing with book business?

Less than five percent.

Which came first, the book or the publisher?

The book.

How did you find a publisher?

I set up a publishing firm to publish my book. I made cursory inquiries to publishers and was not surprised to learn of their lack of interest. This is a specialized field. I also decided to self-publish to maintain complete editorial control.

What was the most valuable thing you learned in your research process?

Thousands of books are published each year. Getting noticed is a major hurdle.

What's it like dealing with your publisher?

Not applicable.

If you set up your own publishing company, please explain the steps you took. Would you do it again?

I set up my own publishing company because I expected to publish more than one book. If one book is the goal, use a vanity publisher to self-publish.

Despite my experience as a writer, magazine editor and feature editor, I needed to hire professionals to make my book presentable. I used a book shepherd[23] to identify a cover designer, book designer, copy editor, promotional writer and printer.

Who did the technical stuff (copyright, ISBN, cover art, editing)?

---

[23] Publishing consultant who provides assistance with such things as cover and book design, editing, finding a printer, production, distribution, marketing and publicity.

My book shepherd also told me how to do the technical stuff of publishing and distribution.

Do you have a merchant account? How do you get paid for your book?

I took orders through my website. I set up necessary connections to accept credit card payments. Eventually I stopped accepting credit card payments and instructed buyers to send a check for a book.

Describe your market and how you reach them.

I mistakenly assumed my book would have appeal to a broad audience. I wasted time and money trying to market to consumers through conventional channels.

For a time after release of my book, I viewed myself as an author and publisher and harbored secret hopes of a popular book. When I recast myself as a financial advisor/expert in a specialized field, then it became clearer to me to market to niche targets: legal, financial and health care professionals.

If starting out now, what would you do different?

Write a book to establish my professional credentials instead of looking to make money on book sales.

What's the best advice you can give someone wanting to sell his or her first book?

Have something significant to say. If writing is not your forte, hire a writer. Have a clear purpose for writing a book.

Irene M. Tomkinson, MSW
Co-Founder Pathways to Personal Growth/Writer/Workshop Facilitator/Life Coach
North Hampton, NH

Tell us about your business.

I am a therapist and workshop and retreat leader.

Tell us about your book(s).

Memoir/self help: Not Like My Mother – Becoming a Sane Parent After Growing Up in a CRAZY Family.

Do you have a dedicated website for your book(s)? What's the address?

Yes. www.Irenetomkinson.com

What percentage of time do you spend each month dealing with book business?

Sometime everyday, some days more than others. 25%

Which came first, the book or the publisher?

The book – I published Print On Demand.

How did you find a publisher?

On line – asking others about their experience, talking to traditional publishers, reading books on publishing and talking to people who had self-published.

What was the most valuable thing you learned in your research process?

I am still learning! I guess the most valuable thing has been how much the industry is changing and that traditional publishing is not the wave of the future….that all publishing is redefining itself.

What's it like dealing with your publisher?

Easy - but I had to know from the get-go that I was responsible for staying on top of everything.

I know that with a traditional publisher I would not have had the control I have, and I would also have to stay on top of the marketing!

If you set up your own publishing company, please explain the steps you took. Would you do it again?

N/A

Who did the technical stuff (copyright, ISBN, cover art, editing)?

The cover art I contracted out to an experienced illustrator.

I contracted out the editing. The ISBN and printing I contracted with Author House Publishers (POD).

Do you have a merchant account? How does that work?

Do you mean do I sell from my own website or through AuthorHouse? I do both. AuthorHouse sells through their site, Barnes & Noble and Amazon.com.

Describe your market and how you reach them.

Ahhh the hard part! I do workshops through churches and schools and my own counseling center, and friends set me up. Anywhere I can, I do workshops with and about the book. This is the best advertising and point of sales. But I am working on pushing people to my website. The book has been out since April (5 months at the time of this interview) and everyday I try to do some marketing and learning about marketing -- the hardest and most elusive part of the whole project.

If starting out now, what would you do differently?

I would not waste a year trying to get a traditional publisher. I would have gone directly to POD printing. With a workshop, along with the book, I think I have a better shot at marketing and maybe later getting picked up by a traditional publisher, if I want that at all. They control so much of the process. I am not sure it would serve me.

What's the best advice you can give someone wanting to sell his or her first book?

Writing my first and only book, <u>Not Like My Mother – Becoming a Sane Parent After Growing Up in a CRAZY Family</u>, was a personal growth experience. I expected that. What I didn't expect was the big growth experience that was to follow - that would be called the "marketing and selling" of my book.

It will be a year in April since the publication. I have done many things to sell my book...workshops, conferences, church talks, given lots of copies away…just look at my credit card bill...some to celebrities ...many to therapists, teachers, agency people, anyone who has any kind of connection to parenting or publishing. And with all this effort I have not, as you may have noticed, become a household name. So far Oprah hasn't called.

What is difficult is to not run in twenty different directions at once. Charging after every little lead or web seminar suggestion or trying to copy the latest idea that has hurled some other author to the top of the NY Times list.

As I enter my second year since publication I am beginning to calm down and gain some grounding. Two main themes for my marketing have begun to emerge.

Marketing a book is a marathon – NOT a sprint. The bad news is I have to be patient and persistent. The good news is that the journey has taken me to places and to people that I would otherwise never have experienced.

I have learned the difference between enrolling people into the ideas of my book and selling them a copy. I love enrolling. I love sharing the concept of a new paradigm for parenting for people who grew up in crazy families. I get energized by enrolling people into my seminars and teaching them how to detach from their histories so that they can be present to their own lives.

Someone once said that writers don't write because they have the answers – they write because they have the questions. And from the questions, through the writing they gain the answers. I have learned that effective marketing for me is sharing my answers.

Roy T. Diliberto, CFP®, CLU, ChFC
RTD Financial Advisors, Inc.
Bonita Springs, FL

Tell us about your business.

We have a comprehensive financial life planning practice. All of our clients go through this process, which involves about 5 meetings initially, periodic meetings when necessary, and an annual "renewal" meeting.

Tell us about your book(s).

Financial Planning – The Next Step: A Practical Approach to Merging Your Clients' Money With Their Lives details our entire planning process, including specific questions to ask, as well as how to organize a financial life planning process, compensating employees, service, etc.

Do you have a dedicated website for your book(s)? What's the address?

No, it is on the Financial Planning Association's (FPA) website with other books published by FPA Press.

What percentage of time do you spend each month dealing with book business?

Only at speaking engagements (approximately 6 each year).

Which came first, the book or the publisher?

The book.

How did you find a publisher?

FPA active member.

What was the most valuable thing you learned in your research process?

Not all quotes that are found on the Internet are accurate and require more digging to get them right.

What's it like dealing with your publisher?

They were helpful with their encouragement and in marketing to their members.

If you set up your own publishing company, please explain the steps you took. Would you do it again?

N/A

Who did the technical stuff (copyright, ISBN, cover art, editing)?

The publisher.

Do you have a merchant account? How does that work?

No.

Describe your market and how you reach them.

Mostly through my speaking engagements. I require that the organization purchase a minimum of 100 books as my "fee" for speaking.

If starting out now, what would you do differently?

Get a marketing plan in writing from the publisher.

What's the best advice you can give someone wanting to sell his or her first book?

Understand your market and choose a publisher who is best equipped to reach that market.

Sheila McCurdy
Certified Professional Organizer
Clutter Stop®
Upland, CA

Tell us about your business.

I am a Certified ADHD[24] Coach, Certified Professional Organizer, author and seminar speaker. My specialty is helping coach and organize people who have Attention Deficit Disorder (ADD), dyslexia, learning disabilities and hoarding issues. These are the subjects that I write and speak about.

Tell us about your book(s).

This book, The Floor is Not an Option!, takes you from the front door and leads you through every room of the house. Along the way you discover ways to handle the clutter that finds its way into every nook and cranny of your house. Once all the clutter is tak-

---

[24] Attention Deficit Hyperactivity Disorder.

en care of you are then shown how to handle all the paper that you are bombarded with every day. You learn what to keep, what to throw away, what to shred, how to set up a filing system, how to file and when to file. And when you are done, any guilt over clutter is gone!

Do you have a dedicated website for your book(s)? What's the address?

www.clutterstop.com

What percentage of time do you spend each month dealing with book business?

At the beginning of writing a book, once it has been published, you do spend quite a bit of time with PR and trying to market the book. There are radio interviews, TV interviews, book signings, etc. It takes a lot of energy and time, so you have to be prepared. It is also a lot of fun.

Which came first, the book or the publisher?

The book came first. I didn't think about the publisher. I just knew that I had to write the book. The first edition was written in 2000.

How did you find a publisher?

I am the publisher. I decided to do self-publishing after a disappointing stint in 2000 at trying to find a publisher only to be told that no one was interested in books aimed at clutter. I don't happen to agree as I believe, and see, that most people have a clutter issue of one sort or another.

What was the most valuable thing you learned in your research process?

Between 2000 and 2008 many things have changed. POD is more in use and a publisher is becoming less the norm, unless you're of the Chicken Soup for the Soul author type.

What's it like dealing with your publisher.

My publisher is wonderful (because it's me!). My current POD company, however, leaves much to be desired. I unfortunately got hooked up with BookSurge who happens to be connected with Amazon. Well, lots of luck, my fellow authors, since I have been waiting since early August for my book order, and as of this date, October 6th, they have not yet arrived. I got books quicker going through a regular printer! I was even told that because I was an author/publisher and got my books wholesale, I was going to have to wait for my books and that if I wanted them any faster I could buy them retail from Amazon! But, good news! I could get royalty payments from it! Wow! Royalty payments from buying my own books at retail. What a thrill! I am already in negotiations with another POD company who lists, very openly, who their board of directors are on their website and how to contact them. BookSurge does not. You have no way of contacting anyone until they contact you. I should have seen the writing on the wall.

As of the printing date of this book, The Floor is Not an Option! is available directly from Amazon or from my website, www.clutterstop.com. I am now with Lightning Source completely, who fulfills all my book orders from Amazon, who is proving easier to work with.

If you set up your own publishing company, please explain the steps you took. Would you do it again?

It takes time. You have to know people – or people who know people. Yes, I would do it again. I prefer knowing what is going on with my book than letting someone else take charge of it. The steps are varied but can be:

1. Find an editor – one you can meet with face to face – how much experience do they have? Do they know how to index?

2. Find a graphics person – also someone you can meet with face to face. How much experience do they have? Have they done a book before? Can they do internal photos if necessary for your book?

Between these two that's pretty much it. You write, one edits, the other puts it into the book graphically. Then you find a POD company when you're ready to print the book. Do your research on this!

Who did the technical stuff (copyright, ISBN, cover art, editing)?

There was a combination on this. Back in 2000 during my first edition book, I got a block of ten ISBN numbers (all that you could do back then). By having that block of ten, I now own my ISBNs, which is a good thing because my POD company cannot say that THEY own the book! I would highly suggest that YOU own your own ISBN numbers.

The copyright language was taken out of other books and my information was put in the appropriate places. It's pretty much standard text.

My Graphic Artist, Donna McClenahan of Graphics via Donna[25], did the cover art and Millie Hinkle did the editing.

---

[25] www.GraphicsviaDonna.com

Do you have a merchant account? How does that work?

I have PayPal set up on my website to handle orders on my site. It's wonderful. Since the new book has just come up, I haven't set it up yet for that but it is currently set up to take orders for the first edition. You go to my website and pay for the book via PayPal. I get the order and mail it off. There is a small processing fee to me for this service, but no monthly fee. If no one buys, I pay nothing to PayPal.

Because of the POD, I was hoping that the way it would work would be that the orders would go through my website and then directly to Amazon who would then mail them off. Since there will now be a break with the POD I will probably be mailing them from my website for a short while until a new POD process is completed.

When I was working with clients, years ago, I used to have a merchant account but so few clients wanted to use a credit card that I finally gave up the account. Having a merchant account was costly. There was a monthly fee, a transaction fee, and a unit fee for the machine. I just didn't see the advantage.

However, since some clients insist on paying by credit card and since I sell books at seminars and workshops where people want to use a credit card, I've opened a new merchant account through First National Merchant Solutions, who can be reached at 800.228.2443. I went through Publishers Marketing Association and received a discount. The machine itself cost me nothing, which was a big factor in going with this company because the others charge you rent. The fees are pretty basic, but less than what I've paid in the past.

Describe your market and how you reach them.

My market is pretty varied, but since my clientele are mostly ADHD and hoarders I advertised on all the ADD sites, and other organizer's websites. I also belong to the National Association of Professional Organizers and the National Study Group on Chronic Disorganization, so I get referrals from them also. Most of my referrals come from these sources and from my clients. I am pretty much a referral-based business.

If starting out now, what would you do differently?

Not use BookSurge!!!

What's the best advice you can give someone wanting to sell his or her first book?

Find yourself a cheerleader. Someone who truly believes in your book and will talk it up for you, everywhere and anywhere. I am fortunate that this time around I have a cheerleader who is acting as my PR agent. She totally believes in the value of the book and what it means for those who hoard, clutter, are ADD and need help.

Richard E. Vodra, JD, CFP®
Spire Investment Partners, LLC
McLean, VA

Tell us about your business.

I've been a Financial Planning Practitioner for 24 years, working with individuals mostly. I have a solo practice, operating in a company that supports me and other practices.

Tell us about your book(s).

I published Enough Money! in 2001. It is 150 pages, directed toward a general, not professional, audience.

Do you have a dedicated website for your book(s)? What's the address?

No.

What percentage of time do you spend each month dealing with book business?

At this point, zero.

Which came first, the book or the publisher?

The book.

How did you find a publisher?

I self-published through Xlibris[26]. I had an agent who marketed the book to several commercial publishers, but without success, so I went with Xlibris.

What was the most valuable thing you learned in your research process?

The most valuable things I learned were

(a) How hard it is to get a commercial publisher interested in a book, even with a good agent, if you aren't already famous,

(b) How easy mechanically it is to self-publish and obtain an attractive product at a reasonable cost, through a print-on-demand firm, and

---

26 www.Xlibris

(c) How hard it is to market a self-published book. I believe that most self-published books are either marketing tools for other purposes (handouts to impress current and potential clients), collateral products to add revenue to other efforts (seminar speakers, etc), or avenues to disappointment if you really expect to sell thousands of copies. People who have an available market, a distribution network they can use, and a valuable and new unique product (like Nancy's first book on becoming a planner) might succeed. Others will have a tough time.

The other thing I learned is that it is really cool to hold a book that you've written, and it's valuable to have something to say you feel so strongly about that you'll put it in a book and be accountable for it.

What's it like dealing with your publisher.

They've had several business models and lots of turnover. It took longer than I expected to get a book, but I stayed in control of the process.

If you set up your own publishing company, please explain the steps you took. Would you do it again?

N/A

Who did the technical stuff (copyright, ISBN, cover art, editing)?

Xlibris did the ISBN number and the copyright (which I own). I did the front cover concept and worked with a graphics person I found for execution. Xlibris has templates and levels of service and I worked with their model.

Do you have a merchant account? How does that work?

Xlibris handles print-on-demand. They also used to sell through Amazon, but Amazon's now changed its policies, so that no longer works.

Describe your market and how you reach them.

I hoped to get some general interest, but didn't. The book is used effectively with clients. Actual sales covered my costs and little more. Good marketing tool, good book, but few independent sales.

If starting out now, what would you do differently?

Depends on what I was trying to do. If I wanted to write a book to express my views,

I'd make a brief inquiry on whether there was a specialty publishing house interested in it. Otherwise, I might set up a blog, outline the book on the blog, see if there's interest, use the comments as free editorial help, self-publish, and see if it could be marketed on the web. If I just wanted to write a book, I'd take my expertise to some publishing houses, see what they're interested in, and write to their specs.

What's the best advice you can give someone wanting to sell his or her first book?

Have a clear idea of why you want to write a book: boost your practice, see your name in print, be recognized as an expert, make a lot of money, get your ideas "out there".

Unless you are unique and marketable or already famous, it's hard to sell a book to a publisher or to get people to buy it.

Self-publishing (or paying a small press to publish for you) your first book can make you more credible to sell your second book. Tom Clancy and Ric Edelman both used that strategy.

Janet Tyler Johnson, CFP®
JATAJ Life Planning, LLC
Blanchardville, WI

Tell us about your business.

I run a fee-only financial planning and investment management (RIA) firm (JATAJ Wealth Management, LLC). I also own a life planning business (JATAJ Life Planning, LLC) through which I sell my book and offer seminars, do public speaking and host workshops.

I am also president of a national network for financial advisors (JATAJ Wealth Advisors Network, LLC) that is a "conference online." The website for this network contains a directory of resources for advisors, free podcasts from industry experts, a list serve that connects advisors to be able to share ideas/challenges, and a free newsletter from yours truly!

All three businesses can be found at www.jataj.com.

Tell us about your book(s).

My book was written for the consumer and/or advisor. It is titled Finding Financial Fulfillment, for a Life Filled with Money and Meaning. It is filled with tips on how to gain clarity about what you really want in life, and then how to use your money to support that vision.

Do you have a dedicated website for your book(s)? What's the address?

No – it can be found at www.jataj.com

What percentage of time do you spend each month dealing with book business?

1-2 hours

Which came first, the book or the publisher?

Publisher

How did you find a publisher?

I took a writing workshop through a local Madison, WI publishing company – they loved my idea for a book and offered to publish it before I even had written a word.

What was the most valuable thing you learned in your research process?

There are many, many ways to get a book from a Word document to a published book. Also, by working with an independent publisher I paid for everything up front and now have no split in royalties. I own 100% of the book and receive 100% of the revenues.

What's it like dealing with your publisher.

This particular publisher was very helpful from everything from the writing phase, design of cover and text, and layout of the book.

If you set up your own publishing company, please explain the steps you took. Would you do it again?

I did not.

Who did the technical stuff (copyright, ISBN, cover art, editing)?

Publisher.

Do you have a merchant account? How does that work?

Yes – I use 1shoppingcart.com. People go to my website, click on the picture of the book, it takes them to the shopping cart where they purchase with a credit card. I then get notified by email that an order has come in. It's all automated as far as the money goes – I receive cash in my checking account within about 3 business days.

Currently, I am the person who mails out the books but I could use a distributor if I chose to pay them.

Describe your market and how you reach them.

My market is both advisors and consumers. I've sold my book at conferences (FPA) to advisors. I do a lot of public speaking and sell books every time I speak.

I also have a free newsletter that I have a link on to buy the book.

If starting out now, what would you do differently?

I might consider self-publishing, as the cost of getting two thousand copies of my book, in soft-cover format, was about $20,000 from start to finish. This includes everything: editing, cover design, book layout, revisions, and printing.

What's the best advice you can give someone wanting to sell his or her first book?

Become a marketing guru. I tried running an ad in RTIR (Radio, TV, Interview Resource) which goes to all radio and TV producers. For about 12 months I averaged about 1.5 interviews a month. Some interviews were great and some were not. But it amounted into almost no sales. They say that the best way to sell on the radio or TV is to have a book signing in the same city that night. I didn't have the time or resources to get those set up, and didn't want to travel all over the country, so I chose to just try radio. It was great media training, and some of the interviews were fun, but since no one around the country had heard of me it didn't get me very many sales.

I do believe that public speaking leads to sales. Once people hear your message they are much more likely to purchase your book.

Ed Jacobson
Edward A. Jacobson Associates
Madison, WI

Tell us about your business.

I'm a psychologist, and I serve the financial planning and related industries and professions through coaching, consulting, training, writing, public speaking, and customized events (client and staff retreats and the like).

Tell us about your book(s).

My one book (thus far) is Appreciative Moments: Stories and Practices for Living and Working Appreciatively. It is a psychology/personal growth book, consisting of short chapters of stories based on my personal and professional experience, from an appreciative, life-affirming, and strength-based perspective. Each story contains between one and five exercises ("Practices" as in the sub-title) for putting the key points of the story into practice in one's life and work.

Do you have a dedicated website for your book(s)? What's the address?

Not specific to the book. However, it is prominently featured on my website, www.edwardjacobson.com. Feel free to visit anytime. :-)

What percentage of time do you spend each month dealing with book business?

At most, 5%.

Which came first, the book or the publisher?

The book. And preceding that were weekly columns, This Appreciative Moment©. Readers began telling me, after the first couple of columns, "Hey, it looks like there's a book in here." That inspired me and I kept it in mind as the months wore on.

How did you find a publisher?

My book coach and writing teacher and friend, Hal Zina Bennett[27] is a world-class author, writing teacher, and consultant to many authors and publishers in the industry. I retained him as my book coach/consultant, and he advised going the print-on-demand route and, within that, he suggested that I use iUniverse[28]. He says that "they are book people" (unlike many other online publishers) and he has used them for as many as 25-30 books (either himself or his coaching clients/writing students). I checked them out, and they worked out well for me, for the most part.

What was the most valuable thing you learned in your research process?

Do what your book coach tells you! (Seriously.) And, like home improvement projects, estimate how long it will take and multiply by three to ten times the estimate.

What's it like dealing with your publisher?

Pretty good, now. They went through a relocation (to a different city) and reassigned my project person without telling me (not good!) and assigned me a total incompetent

27 www.halbooks.com

28 www.iUniverse

(worse). Because Hal has a very close working relationship with the firm, he was able to raise holy you-know-what and get some action. My post-publishing contact with iUniverse has been fine. I'd recommend them, with the proviso that the author have an option to change PSA's (the project person's acronym) if dissatisfied.

If you set up your own publishing company, please explain the steps you took. Would you do it again?

N/A

Who did the technical stuff (copyright, ISBN, cover art, editing)?

That's the beauty of using iUniverse (and perhaps other publishers). They do that stuff, and I gotta tell ya, they produced a GORGEOUS cover for my book…as you know.

Do you have a merchant account? How does that work?

I have a PayPal merchant account, if that's what you're asking. Unfortunately, it's not linked to my website, so at the moment, people can't order my book online and go to order fulfillment/payment. It goes through my director of operations (that would be me).

Describe your market and how you reach them.

Anyone (seriously). For now, it's back-of-room sales and through my columns (distributed to about nine hundred planners and others). I'm not on top of the marketing of the book at present. It's more a calling card for my public speaking work.

If starting out now, what would you do differently?

Nothing comes to mind. It's worked well. Maybe I'd have retained a non-financial industry publicist, to provide a broader launch.

What's the best advice you can give someone wanting to sell his or her first book?

Don't count on its being a best seller, and don't get your ego wrapped up in the sales numbers. Treat each book sale and signing as a gift of grace, from the buyer to you and vice versa. If the "someone" (in your question) were comfortable using a packaged marketing approach (Steve Harrison, prLeads, others), they might go that route. But they should have "people" (someone who knows the industry and knows how to market books) behind them.

Nancy Langdon Jones, CFP®
Financial Planner and Author
Claremont, CA

Tell us about your business.

I'm a financial planner who wrote a book. Having recently retired from financial planning, I'm working on other books.

Tell us about your book(s).

So You Want to Be a Financial Planner: Your Guide to a New Career is a "how to guide" for career changers and students seeking a career in the financial planning profession.

'Specially Not No Chocolate! by Claude Earl Jones is a short fiction piece by my husband that I published as part of the research for this book.

Do you have a dedicated website for your book(s)? What's the address?

Yes: www.nancysbooks.com

What percentage of time do you spend each month dealing with book business?

Far less than I should if I were to market properly. Maybe 5%.

Which came first, the book or the publisher?

The book in both cases. I tried to get a publisher to look at my proposal for So You Want to Be a Financial Planner to no avail. In the case of my husband's book, I told him if he'd write it, I'd publish it.

How did you find a publisher?

I gave up and decided to publish So You Want to Be a Financial Planner myself as an eBook. I did all the work and just as I was ready to publish, I approached AdvisorPress[29], a brand new publishing company that was interested in publishing eBooks. Since my book was ready to go, they offered to co-publish and get me on Amazon, a nearly insurmountable task for an independent in 2001.

What was the most valuable thing you learned in your research process?

Traditional publishing (printing ten thousand books at a time) is obsolete.

What's it like dealing with your publisher.

---

29 www.AdvisorPress

AdvisorPress is wonderful to deal with! Very responsive. Of course we've had our differences from time to time, but they are always willing to negotiate. They are extremely easy to reason with and have come up with excellent suggestions to improve the quality of successive editions. So You Want to Be a Financial Planner is in its fifth edition.

If you set up your own publishing company, please explain the steps you took. Would you do it again?

I used NancysBooks as a publishing company for 'Specially Not No Chocolate! Since I already had the website it seemed a logical thing to do.

First I found a POD (print-on-demand) printer, Lightning Source[30], who also prints So You Want to Be a Financial Planner. It was easy to register NancysBooks with them. Instructions on Lightning Source's website are perfectly clear.

Once the book was ready to upload, it was a snap! Lightning Source takes care of the distribution to Amazon and other booksellers.

Who did the technical stuff (copyright, ISBN, cover art, editing)?

[30] www.lightningsource.com

I copyrighted both books online, sending two copies to the Library of Congress. I got my own ISBN for both books, though LightningSource would have done that. Claude had a photograph he wanted for the cover of 'Specially Not No Chocolate! and we worked with a friend who used Paint Shop to design the cover. I did have problems fitting the cover into the Lightning Source template and hired a graphic artist to help me. That wasthe greatest expense we had ($600). Friends proofread both books. Total outlay for 'Specially Not No Chocolate!, including the graphic artist and the first 100 books, was just over $1000. 'Specially Not No Chocolate! is under 100 pages, so it is inexpensive to print and Lightning Source periodically runs specials.

Do you have a merchant account? How does that work?

NancysBooks has a merchant account with Costco called Elevon. We take American Express, Discover, MasterCard and Visa. We're billed a flat monthly rate plus transaction charges. Buyers who log onto NancysBooks can purchase books by clicking on buttons, which take them to our secure Cartmanager shopping cart. Once the order is placed, the buyer's card is automatically charged, I am sent an email notification of the purchase so I can ship the book and the funds are deposited in my bank account within a day or two.

Describe your market and how you reach them.

My market for So You Want to Be a Financial Planner is career changers and students. I should contact all the schools teaching the CFP course, but in reality have been in touch with relatively few. This marketing stuff is hard work and time consuming.

For 'Specially Not No Chocolate! we sent email notices to a huge list of contacts in our database.

If starting out now, what would you do differently?

AdvisorPress wasn't around when I first started out, but if I were doing it all over again, I would make a beeline for them and let them do all the dirty work! Also, I would take marketing more seriously…it's still not too late!

If my husband wanted to write another book, I'd publish it for him (and learn how to fit the cover to the Lightning Source template myself). Except for the graphics, it was painless!

What's the best advice you can give someone wanting to sell his or her first book?

Understand that writing the book is the easy part. Marketing is the hard part! In between there is publishing and there are wonderful tools available today to allow you to do as much or as little of that part as you wish to do. Enjoy the process or hire someone to help you!

Chapter Seven

Publishers Who (May) Want Your Book

Getting someone to publish your book today is not the daunting task it once was…nor does self-publishing carry the unprofessional stigma it once did.

Still, there is no question a good publisher can take care of a lot of detail so you won't need to. While I ePublished the electronic version of my first book and printed the first few copies at Kinko's at great cost, the final print version was handled by AdvisorPress, working with Lightning Source, and I would not hesitate to hire them again.

Since I didn't originally have a publisher, I did all the scut work of buying ISBNs and downloading bar codes and sending copies to the Copyright Office. Publishers are set up to do this stuff easily.

When I went to Kinko's to have copies made I had a dickens of a time since I had copyrighted the manuscript. Even after explaining and proving that I held the copyright I had to go up the management chain until I found someone bright enough to send me to the commercial printing division where they were used to dealing with original material. The process was costly at that time (2001) and there wasn't much help from the Internet on the topic of self-publishing. Today it's a whole other story. Not only have costs come down, but access to printers and publishers is prolific! Individuals can even get their books straight to Amazon, which was once impossible.

If I were just starting out today, the first thing I would do is purchase Mark Levine's comprehensive book The Fine Print of Self-Publishing: The Contracts & Services of 45 Self-Publishing Companies – Analyzed, Ranked & Exposed[31]. The title says it all. Levine literally takes 45 self-publishing companies and compares their fees, formats, contracts and just about everything else, then gives them an "author-friendly rating" and ranks them from outstanding to dismal. What an eye-opener!

In Chapter 4, titled "The Fine Print of Publishing Contracts", Levine breaks down the parts of a publishing contract and tells you exactly what to look for...and to ask for.

---

[31] Mark Levine's The Fine Print of Self-Publishing, 3rd Edition, Hillcrest Publishing Group, September 2008.

This chapter alone is worth the cost of the book.

Peter Johnson, CEO
Mattias Bergman, COO
AdvisorPress – see the URL
http://www.advisorpress.com/

Tell us about your publishing company, AdvisorPress.

We are a small publisher, focusing on personal finance books for both the professional and the consumer.

From our website:

"AdvisorPress is your premier source for high-royalty publishing services. We understand the specific needs of professional associations, educational institutions and authors. Leveraging our knowledge and experience, we help you make money and enhance your brand using innovative publishing services that are fast, cost-efficient and highly effective.

We've pioneered new processes designed to tear down the barriers to profitably publishing professional books. For example, we help ensure that your cash flow stays positive throughout the process, and that books are profitable even at low sales volumes. We provide distribution through all major retail outlets, on and off-line, in print, eBook, and audio formats. Furthermore, we have partnered with major professional institutions, enabling them to create their own publishing brands, and sell books directly to their own members as well as consumers.

In short, AdvisorPress offers tailored services for increased profitability. It is this knowledgeable, rewarding approach that has led to satisfied partners and best-selling financial books."

What topics are you looking for?

We are interested in non-fiction books on personal finance topics written for consumers, professionals, and sometimes for both groups. "Personal finance" includes such wide-ranging topics as budgeting, retirement, investing, tax issues, estate planning, stock options, family money communication, and the business of personal financial planning itself.

Does the book come first or the publisher?

We feel that the start of the book needs to come first — the author first needs to be motivated to write a book, and to write about a topic that excites him or her. Once the book project has begun, however, then the publisher becomes important. It is always in the author's best interest to contact several publishers, and select one before completing the book. It's best to consider issues such as the audience, marketing, content, approach, and packaging during the book development process, and a publisher can be helpful during this period.

Who owns the copyright on books you publish?

The author owns the copyright. AdvisorPress will assign an ISBN and register the copyright as a service, but the author will always retain their copyright.

Do you market the books you publish?

There are two clear rules about book marketing, especially for non-fiction books:

1. The author needs to drive marketing for his or her book.
2. If there are any questions, see Rule 1.

That being said, AdvisorPress offers numerous marketing opportunities and distribution options to the author. For instance, we have held monthly "Author Marketing Conference Calls" with nationally recognized experts. We have distribution channels into online sellers, all major physical retail channels, professional associations, our own website and even retailers in Europe for those authors who desire it. We have established a "Financial Literacy" partnership with several bookstore chains that is set to go nationwide soon. We provide marketing information, references and introductions to our authors, so that they do not need to start from scratch.

What do you offer the author?

In addition to the marketing and distribution support listed above, we offer one of the most competitive royalty structures in the business, as well as a network of production partners that help reduce the cost of book production to a minimum. We have production and distribution channels that can provide profitable publishing even at extremely low volumes.

How can authors reach you if they have a book or proposal ready?

Our website, http://www.advisorpress.com/, includes contact information that allows authors to reach the business principals directly:

Peter Johnson, CEO, peter@advisorpress.com

Mattias Bergman, COO,

Mattias@advisorpress.com

Lance Ritchlin
Director of Publications
Financial Planning Association

Tell us about your publishing company, FPA Press.

We've been in the book publishing business for about four years, now, and have about a dozen titles in print. Our mission is twofold: To provide information to members of the broad financial planning community that they can't get from other publishers, and to provide opportunities for authors.

What topics are you looking for?

We're interested in books for those involved in financial planning or financial services primarily, especially technical subjects, which FPA Press finds easier to market to financial professionals.

We attend industry conference sessions to see what's out there and approach speakers for new articles and book ideas.

Primary questions we ask are whether it offers information that will be helpful to our members, it represents a unique perspective, and we will be able to market the book and expect it will make money. We take the stewardship of membership dollars very seriously. If we feel we aren't the right publisher or the author has a different profit motive, we'll refer to other publishers.

Does the book come first or the publisher?

Either way. We're just now finding our niche and what our audience will appreciate. We're becoming more pro-active in identifying topics, but are certainly open to pitched ideas.

While submitting a proposal is usually the first step, we'll take a look at a completed manuscript.

Who owns the copyright on books you publish?

That's a decision we make on a case-by-case basis, but generally FPA will hold the copyright. Occasionally we will publish without owning the copyright, but in those cases we will insist on an exclusive license to publish. The books are a great launching pad for other opportunities, such as speaking engagements, magazine articles, seminars, blogs and our practice management site. Some of our authors donate royalties to the Foundation for Financial Planning.

Do you market the books you publish?

We market to members, offer the book to media through public relations efforts, and reach external audiences to the best of our ability, including offering the books to libraries and Amazon.com. Some titles may go into bricks and mortar stores. The book establishes the author as a content expert, but ultimately, marketing is a partnership between the publisher and the author, and requires the best efforts of both parties.

What do you offer the author?

We work collaboratively with our authors. We want the author's support as a true partner.

To accomplish this, we establish the roles so the author is comfortable knowing who is doing what. We are responsive and email promptly during the implementation period.

We have a standard royalty agreement with the author, and FPA Press takes care of all the technical details like cover graphics, printing, copyrighting, etc. We determine a print quantity based on our understanding of the market for the book, but as a short-run printer, we have the flexibility to meet demand as it develops.

We're also open to creative arrangements with the author, including special projects and company underwriting to have additional books available for distribution to employees.

How can authors reach you if they have a book or proposal ready?

They can contact us with book proposals at FPApress@FPAnet.org, or speak with the managing editor by phone at 800.322.4237, ext.7143.

Patricia H. Troy, President
Bay Media, Inc.
Severna Park, MD

Tell us about your publishing company, Bay Media, Inc.

I started the company in 1989 to focus on community publications. We have now expanded to include books, booklets, brochures, and Web sites. We refer to ourselves as a publication management company.

Many of our clients come from the non-profit community, but also include small businesses and individuals. I also own an association management firm and we serve the publication need of the management firm's clients.

For books, we offer what we call "cooperative publishing." This pricing model is essentially the same as we use for our other print and Web publications.

The book must meet our standards for acceptance. This means it must be well written, accurate (if non-fiction) and marketable (to a general or niche audience). We will not publish porn or anything we consider to be in poor taste, politically inflammatory, or contain information that is not reliable. If the book is something we can be proud to put our logo on, we will develop a proposal.

Basically, we charge the client for our time (consultation, design, editing, project management) and the printing (which we markup). The client owns the books once they are published.

What topics are you looking for?

We do not limit the topics we accept, however, many of the books we publish are local history, children's books, and books for niche markets.

Does the book come first or the publisher?

We do not advertise our services, with the exception of our Web site. Most referrals come via word of mouth. Authors contact us directly, usually after having made the decision NOT to attempt to deal with a conventional publisher.

Who owns the copyright on books you publish?

Typically, the author retains copyright. In some instances we have a shared copyright, but we are moving away from that practice.

Do you market the books you publish?

Our basic contract includes registration with Bowker and a distributor/wholesaler (typically Baker and Taylor). We encourage authors to register directly with Amazon.com. We often will design and print marketing materials under a separate contract. If needed, we can arrange for public relations and marketing assistance, but that is not part of our standard package. Our authors generally prefer to do their own marketing. In this economic climate, direct sales (outside of bookstores) seem to be the most effective ways for our authors to market their books.

What do you offer the author?

We serve as the publisher, imprinting with our logo. Much of what we offer is experience, advice and expertise. We design the cover (using a professional illustrator) and layout the book (using our staff graphic designer). Of course, we supply the ISBN and register with Bowker and also Baker and Taylor. We get competitive pricing quotes on the printing (we have many options) and handle everything associated with managing the printing process. If the book is printed outside of the US, we work with a customs broker. As an option, we can produce public relations and marketing materials, set up Web sites, and provide marketing services. Our contracts vary with the needs of the client.

How can authors reach you if they have a book or proposal ready?

Pat@baymed.com
Bay Media, Inc.
550M Ritchie Highway, #271
Severna Park, MD 21146
410-647-8402

Chapter Eight

The Big Picture: A Checklist

It's easy to get lost in the myriad of things necessary to get your book to market. Here I've provided a checklist of items to remember. Many of these things can be done simultaneously and in any order, but, at some, time you'll probably have to address most of them.

☐ Book Idea

This is the starting place, of course. You need to know that you want to write a book and have an idea that you feel will sell. Dare to dream a little here and do some research before finalizing your decision; then get started!

☐ **Write Proposal**

Your proposal will help you focus and keep on track as you proceed. It is the most important initial step you can take. You'll create a roadmap of sorts, giving yourself direction and incentive.

☐ **Find Publisher**

Maybe it's you! There is no reason today why it shouldn't be, with a plethora of printers and other professionals at your disposal. But if you anticipate having a professional publisher, now's the time to begin looking…well before you've written much.

☐ **Write**

You've already started if you've written a proposal, and if not on paper, you certainly have ideas of what you want to say. Do what you have to do to get the book written, and that generally means, write every chance you get.

☐ **Format**

Decide what your book will look like. Will it be hardbound or soft cover? Normal paperback size or coffee table size? Pictures or graphics included? Choosing the layout and fonts up front and using them consistently will save time and work later.

☐ **Proofreaders/Editor**

Students, especially English majors, make wonderful proofreaders. You'll need at least a couple, more if your book is of a technical nature. You may want to hire an editor to review your book for content, consistency and overall recommendations.

☐ **Printer**

If you're publishing your book yourself, you'll need a good printer who has contacts to get your book out to bookstores and online markets.

☐ **ISBN/Barcode**

Most printers and/or publishers should be able to provide you with an ISBN with digital barcode. If not, you can purchase your own directly from sources on the Internet.

☐ **Seller's Permit**

Check out the state sales tax in the location(s) from which you'll be selling your book(s). Generally you'll need to charge sales tax only for print books you sell in the same state in which you're selling/sending the book. No sales tax for electronic books…yet.

☐ **Cover Art**

Your printer should have specific templates for submitting cover art. The difficult part is finding or designing the cover you want. The back cover generally contains benefits of buying your book, information about you and maybe brief quotes from those who have read your book.

☐ **Proof Out for Comment**

Once you have copy that can be sent, get it out to friends and colleagues with a cover letter asking for comments. Hopefully you'll receive glowing reviews to quote on your back cover and publicity material.

☐ **Foreword**

If you know or can find an important, well-regarded authority in the subject of your book, contact them with a proof copy and ask if they would do you the honor of writing a foreword. Ask permission to include their name, perhaps on the front cover to increase sales.

☐ **Website**

Will you be selling your book from your own new dedicated website or from a website you already have set up? In either case, you'll need special copy explaining to visitors how they can purchase your book.

☐ **PayPal and/or Merchant Account**

If you plan on selling your book online from your website and will be taking credit cards, you'll need a PayPal or a Merchant Account and a shopping cart. Your bank, Costco, and online services can provide the information you need to get started.

☐ Print Book

Obviously, you'll actually need the print book! Once the proof is perfect, send the final copy to the printer and place your first order. There is nothing quite like getting that first box of books that you have authored!

☐ Copyright

As soon as a print copy of your book is available, send it (electronically or by mail) to the U. S. Government Copyright office to be registered. Hey! You wrote it, you don't want anyone else taking credit!

☐ Mailing List

Maybe this should have been number one on the list. In any case, an up-to-date mailing list (email and snail mail) is imperative! Check yours and get your flyers ready! Time to get the word out!

☐ Flyer

Even if you're not carrying boxes of your book around in the trunk of your car, you'll want to have something to give to prospective buyers, which includes anyone in earshot, when the topic comes up. (It's up to you to make certain the topic comes up!) Design something with all the pertinent facts, including where and how to buy the book. Consider printing up bookmarks with the necessary information.

☐ **Amazon**

Many printers and publishers have contracts with Amazon, Barnes & Noble, Ingram and other outlets and will notify them that your book is ready for sale. If you need to contact Amazon yourself, go to their website and follow the instructions. Good luck! Remember to put your book in Kindle[32] format on Amazon!

☐ **Copies to Media**

Send copies of your book to newspapers, TV and radio stations with a nice cover letter asking them to write a review or to interview you. Follow up!

☐ **Copies to Contributors**

Remember to send complimentary autographed copies to all the wonderful people who have helped you with your book: proofreaders, people you quote, reviewers, etc.

☐ **Enjoy!**

---

[32] Amazon's electronic book

Resources

Aiming at Amazon: The NEW Business of Self Publishing by Aaron Shepard, Shepard Publications, 2007.

Book Design and Production: A Guide for Authors and Publishers by Pete Masterson, Aenix Publishing Group, 2007.

The Clearly Confusing World of Self-Publishing & POD by Clea Saal, virtual-bookworm.com, 2003.

The Complete Guide to Self-Publishing by Tom & Marilyn Ross, Writer's Digest Books, 2002.

ePublishing for Dummies® by Victoria Rosenborg, IDG Books Worldwide, Inc., 2001.

The Fast Track Course on How to Write a Nonfiction Book Proposal by Stephen Blake Mettee, Quill Driver Books/Word Dancer Press, Inc., 2002.

The Fine Print of Self-Publishing: The Contracts & Services of 45 Major Self-Publishing Companies – Analyzed, Ranked & Exposed by Mark Levine, Hillcrest Publishing Group, 2008.

The Frugal Book Promoter: How to Do What Your Publisher Won't by Carolyn Howard-Johnson, Star Publish, 2004.

The Frugal Editor: Put Your Best Book Forward to Avoid Humiliation and Ensure Success by Carolyn Howard-Johnson, Red Engine Press, 2007.

Plug Your Book! Online Book Marketing for Authors by Steve Weber, Weber Books, 2007.

Print-On-Demand Book Publishing by Morris Rosenthal, Foner Books, 2004.

Self-Publishing Manual: How to Write, Print and Sell Your Own Book by Dan Poynter, Para Publishing, 2007.

Sell Your Book on Amazon: Top-Secret Tips Guaranteed to Increase Sales for Print-On-Demand and Self-Publishing Writers by Brent Sampson, Outskirts Press, 2007.

The Well-Fed Self-Publisher: How to Turn One Book into a Full-Time Living by Peter Bowerman, Fanove Publishing, 2007

Index

A

B

C

D

E

F

G

H

I

J

K

L

M

N

O

P

R

S

T

V

W

X

About the Author

Nancy Langdon Jones is a CFP® licensee and author of So You Want to Be a Financial Planner: Your Guide to a New Career.

She and her husband, actor/director Claude Earl Jones, live in Claremont, California.

LaVergne, TN USA
12 January 2010
169711LV00005B/98/P

9 781603 530170